COUNTRIES IN OUR WORLD

UNITED KINGDOM

Michael Burgan

W
FRANKLIN WATTS
LONDON•SYDNEY

This edition published in 2013 by
Franklin Watts
338 Euston Road
London NW1 3BH

Franklin Watts Australia
Level 17/207 Kent Street
Sydney NSW 2000

 Produced for Franklin Watts by
White-Thomson Publishing Ltd
+44 (0) 845 362 8240
www.wtpub.co.uk

Series consultant: Rob Bowden
Editor: Sonya Newland
Designer: Amy Sparks
Picture researcher: Sonya Newland

A CIP catalogue record for this book is available
from the British Library.

Dewey Classification: 941'.086

ISBN 978 1 4451 1897 0

Printed in Malaysia

Franklin Watts is a division of Hachette Children's
Books, an Hachette UK company

www.hachette.co.uk

Contents

The United Kingdom is one of the most developed countries in the world. Although small in size, it once controlled an empire that included a quarter of the world's land and people. Today the country has only a few overseas colonies, but its global influence remains strong.

Where in the world?

The United Kingdom is an island off the north-western coast of mainland Europe. It is made up of four countries: England, Scotland, Wales and Northern Ireland. These are ruled by a central government in the English capital, London, but the other three countries have some powers of self-rule. Apart from the land border between Northern Ireland and the independent Republic of Ireland, the UK is surrounded by water.

Nations coming together

The United Kingdom rose out of the growing strength of England. During the thirteenth century, English armies defeated those in neighbouring Wales.

▲ *The UK is surrounded by the Atlantic Ocean, the North Sea, the English Channel and the Irish Sea. Its closest neighbours on the continent of Europe are France, Norway and the Netherlands.*

The English tried to take over Scotland as well, but the Scottish resisted. The two kingdoms finally united peacefully in 1707 under the name Great Britain. The British also controlled Ireland, and when the Irish gained independence in 1921, Northern Ireland remained part of the United Kingdom.

IT'S A FACT!

The term United Kingdom refers to England, Scotland, Wales and Northern Ireland. The name Great Britain only includes England, Scotland and Wales. The British Isles is the name given to Great Britain, Ireland and other smaller islands, such as the Channel Islands of Guernsey and Jersey.

A world power

Throughout its history, the UK has had far-reaching connections with other countries. Over the centuries, the British gained control of many distant lands and eventually ruled a vast empire. Ships brought natural resources from faraway places, and British factories turned those materials into goods that were sold around the world. British people also settled in the colonies, taking with them their language, art, religions and customs, and helping British culture spread throughout the world. Although virtually all the colonies are now independent, many of them have kept cultural and political ties with the UK.

▼ *The UK has a central government based at the Houses of Parliament in London, but Scotland, Wales and Northern Ireland also have their own national governments.*

International relations

The United Kingdom remains close to most of its former colonies and dominions. Many of them belong to the Commonwealth of Nations, an organization formed by the UK in 1931. Its members work together to promote shared goals around the world, such as democracy, equal rights, free trade and world peace. The United States is one of the UK's closest allies, and the two nations fought together during World War I (1914–18) and World War II (1939–45). Today, they are major trading partners and often act along similar lines when combating global terrorism and other problems.

GOING GLOBAL

The English language is one of the UK's greatest exports. Today, more than 40 nations use it as their official language, and about 350 million people speak it as their first language. Experts estimate that around one billion people are currently learning English.

▼ *US president Barack Obama and former British prime minister Gordon Brown. The UK and USA have close political ties.*

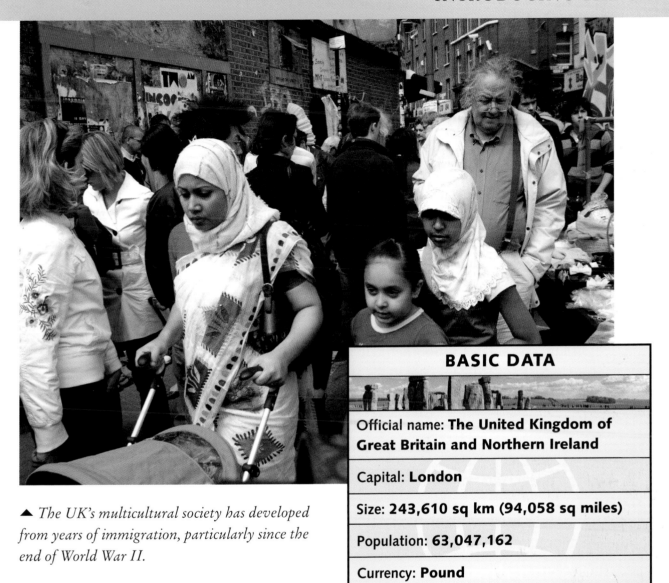

▲ *The UK's multicultural society has developed from years of immigration, particularly since the end of World War II.*

BASIC DATA	
Official name: The United Kingdom of Great Britain and Northern Ireland	
Capital: **London**	
Size: **243,610 sq km (94,058 sq miles)**	
Population: **63,047,162**	
Currency: **Pound**	

Looking ahead

Despite its wealth, the UK faces some tough challenges. The population is expected to grow by about six million people by 2020, partly because of the large numbers of immigrants settling in the UK. They will need education, jobs and services such as healthcare, and the government will need to find ways of paying for these. Not everyone in the UK welcomes immigrants, fearing they will take away jobs and housing.

The government hopes to provide for everyone's needs and end any tension between the immigrants and citizens. The UK is also facing competition in selling its goods and services in global markets, especially from countries such as China and India, which are developing strong economies. Government officials hope that by promoting education and new ideas in science and technology, the UK can continue to be a global influence.

Landscapes and environment

Almost completely surrounded by water, the United Kingdom is made up of hundreds of islands. The biggest, Great Britain, covers 229,979 sq km (88,795 sq miles) and is the eighth-largest island in the world. Island groups off the coast include the Shetlands, Orkneys and Hebrides.

Highlands and hills

A large part of the UK is covered with hills and low mountains. The Scottish Highlands, to the north, are home to Ben Nevis, the UK's highest peak at 1,343 m (4,406 ft). The Southern Uplands stretch to the border with England, which is marked by the Cheviot Hills. The Pennines, another range of hills, run from north to south across the border, reaching into central England and forming a kind of 'backbone' through the central UK. The country's hills and mountains continue into Wales – where the Cambrians are the main mountain range – and Northern Ireland also has several small mountain ranges. Rocky cliffs dot the coastline all round the country.

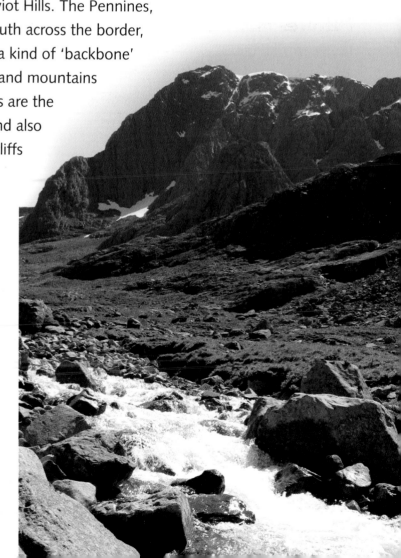

PLACE IN THE WORLD

Total area: 243,610 sq km (94,058 sq miles)

Percentage of world land area: 0.16%

World ranking: 79th

▶ *Ben Nevis stands in the Grampian Mountains, in the Scottish Highlands.*

Pastures and meadows

The heart of England is much flatter than the lands to the west and north. Rolling hills covered with pastures and meadows ring many cities and towns, and some more isolated areas are covered in moorland. The damp land of many moors supports a variety of grasses and heather.

 The Severn Bridge connects England and Wales where they are separated by the River Severn.

Rivers and lakes

Rivers flow through all parts of the UK. The longest is the River Severn at 354 km (220 miles), which starts in the Cambrian Mountains and flows westwards into the Bristol Channel. To the east, the Thames flows from Gloucestershire to the North Sea, a distance of 340 km (211 miles). Other important rivers include the Trent and Great Ouse. The Lake District, in north-west England, is famous for its beautiful landscapes and is a popular tourist destination. Here, 14 main lakes and many smaller ones sit among mountains up to 975 m (3,200 ft) high. The UK's largest freshwater lake, Lough Neagh, lies in the middle of Northern Ireland.

IT'S A FACT!

The world's oldest insect fossil was discovered in Scotland in 1919. This ancient insect was fossilized in rock about 400 million years ago, although only parts of its jaw remain. The fossil is now owned by London's Natural History Museum.

Climate

The UK climate is temperate, which means that the temperature does not usually drop sharply in winter or soar in summer. The warm ocean waters of the Gulf Stream help keep the islands relatively warm and free of snow during most winters. In summer, sea breezes keep the country cool. London has an average January high temperature of 7°C (44°F). In July, the average high is 23°C (73°F). In general, temperatures are highest in the south and coolest in the Highlands of Scotland. Rainfall is high all over the UK, but the west coast gets more rain than the east. London has an average rainfall of 59 cm (23 in) per year.

▼ *Flooding can be a problem in the UK, bringing misery to many. Extreme rainfall may be on the increase.*

GOING GLOBAL

The Giant's Causeway in Northern Ireland is one of the UK's best-known World Heritage Sites – places selected by the international organization UNESCO for their natural beauty or their cultural and historical significance. The remains of lava that flowed about 60 million years ago, the causeway has about 40,000 stone columns grouped closely together along the shore. Rapid cooling of the lava shaped most of the stones into hexagons (with six sides), although some have fewer sides, some more.

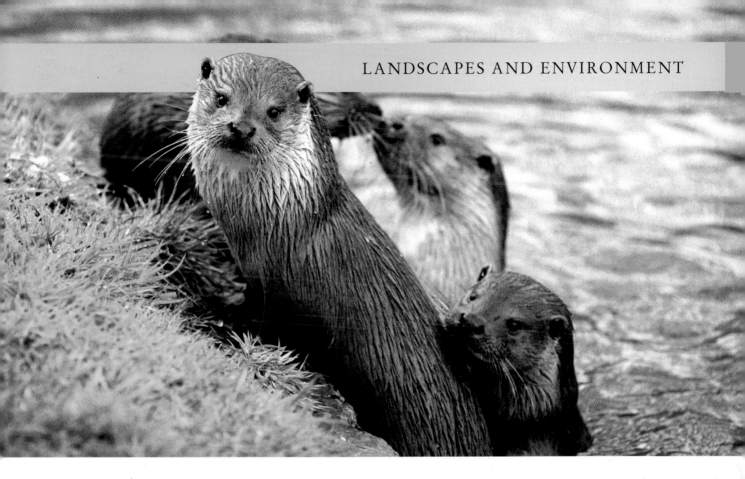

Environmental issues

Like many countries, the UK faces several environmental issues. Cars and factories cause air pollution, and waste from industry is polluting the waters. The UK has taken several steps towards addressing environmental problems, though. It has met the targets set by the international Kyoto agreement for reducing greenhouse-gas emissions, but there is still much work to be done in the UK in tackling pollution and climate change.

Wildlife

Hundreds of animal species make their homes in the UK's waterways and sea shores, including otters, various reptiles and amphibians, and sea birds. The country's forests and fields also have a great variety of

▲ *Programmes to clean up the UK's waterways have resulted in wildlife such as otters returning to the Thames.*

THE HOME OF...

The Scottish Crossbill

Crossbills - birds of the finch family- can be found in many countries, but in 2006 scientists announced that one species is unique to Scotland. Unlike related species, the Scottish crossbill has a distinct call used to attract a mate. Scientists have called this the bird's 'Scottish accent'.

wildlife, including deer, foxes, rabbits, wildcats and bats. There is only one species of poisonous snake in the UK – the adder; this is the only snake native to Scotland.

Population and migration

Since its days as a global empire, the UK has attracted people from other nations. Today, immigrants from India, Pakistan and many other former colonies contribute to the UK's diverse population.

Who are the British?

Just over 90 per cent of Britons are white. Most people are of English descent, followed by Scottish, Welsh and Northern Irish. Black people make up two per cent of the population, Indians are just under two per cent and Pakistanis make up 1.3 per cent. The remaining Britons are of mixed background or other ethnic origin.

▼ *At school, children are taught about different religions and cultural backgrounds.*

GOING GLOBAL

In 2011, these were the top ten countries of origin for new settlers to the UK, shown by percentage of all new settlers:

India	19%	South Africa	3%
Pakistan	9%	Zimbabwe	3%
China	5%	Bangladesh	3%
Philippines	5%	Somalia	3%
Nigeria	4%	United States	3%

PLACE IN THE WORLD

Population: **63,047,162**

Percentage of world total: **0.89%**

World ranking: **22nd**

Where do they live?

England has the largest population of the four countries of the UK, with more than 53 million inhabitants. Most live in the central and eastern regions, particularly in and around the largest cities: London, Birmingham, Leeds, Sheffield, Bradford, Liverpool and Manchester. Scotland has just over 5.3 million people, most centred around its capital Edinburgh, and the second-largest city Glasgow. The population of Wales is just over three million, while Northern Ireland has over 1.8 million people.

Population growth

Across the UK, a rise in the number of births and a decrease in deaths means that the population is rising rapidly. The population increase is also helped by net migration, as more people enter the country from abroad than leave to live in other countries. In 1997, net migration was less than 50,000 people; in 2012, it was more than 183,000.

▲ *Birmingham is the second-largest city in the UK, with a population of over two million.*

Newcomers to the UK

People from other countries in the European Union are allowed to settle freely in the UK. In 2004, ten countries joined the EU, with a further two joining in 2007. Many residents of these nations decided to move to the UK, especially those from Eastern Europe. Tens of thousands of people came from Poland, and several thousand also arrived from Bulgaria and Romania. Others choosing to live in the UK are refugees fleeing wars or other troubles in countries such as Iraq, Afghanistan, Somalia or Zimbabwe.

Immigration issues

The ongoing rise in immigration has sparked a population boom in some towns. Sometimes there is not enough money to provide public services for the newcomers, and schools struggle to teach foreign-born students who speak little or no English. On the other hand, many adult immigrants arrive with college educations and established professions. The challenge for these people is trying to find jobs that match their skills.

IT'S A FACT!

In 2010, the figure for net immigration was at a record high. Although the number of immigrants remained the same as the year before, fewer people decided to emigrate.

◀ *This boy fled with his family from the war in Iraq. He attends evening classes at a special school, which teaches refugee children in their own language.*

Moving within the UK

Many people move around within the borders of the UK. Throughout the twentieth century, hundreds of thousands of people in Scotland and northern England moved south to look for work in cities such as London. However, in 2010 about 250,000 people left London to live in other parts of the country. This reflects a new pattern of city dwellers moving to suburbs or even rural areas far from the cities. They seek more space or want to avoid the crime often found in cities. Technology such as the Internet also means that many jobs can be done outside the cities – even from home – so people do not need to live in the cities to work.

▲ *There are large communities of Britons in countries such as Spain. Some people emigrate when they retire, but others just want a more relaxed lifestyle.*

GOING GLOBAL

Some UK residents choose to move overseas. Although some leave for a short time and then return to their native country, others never return. In 2011, about 350,000 British people emigrated to other countries. Popular destinations for emigrants include the USA, Germany, Spain, Australia and Canada.

Culture and lifestyles

For thousands of years, British culture has been influenced by the different backgrounds of the people who have settled there. More recently, British writers, artists and musicians have created works that are world-famous.

A range of influences

More than 10,000 years ago, settlers came to the British Isles from Europe. In the centuries that followed, the Celts, Romans, different Germanic tribes and other Europeans followed. All brought their own languages, shaping the English that is spoken today. In parts of Scotland, Wales and Northern Ireland, some people still speak languages with Celtic roots.

A religious people

For centuries, most people in the UK were Roman Catholics, but in the sixteenth century the Protestant Church of England became the main religion. Today, Britons follow a variety of Christian faiths, but immigrants from Asia, the Middle East and Africa have brought other religions to the UK, including Islam, Hinduism and Buddhism.

▼ *Hundreds of old churches, like this one in Underbarrow, Cumbria, still stand in villages all over the UK.*

▲ *Bagpipers play at the opening of the Highland Games on the Scottish island of Skye.*

A music-loving people

The cultural variety of the UK is reflected in its music. Folk musicians play songs that are hundreds of years old, and Scotland's famous Highland Games often feature bagpipes. Classical composers such as George Frederic Handel and Benjamin Britten wrote music that is still performed all over the world. Pop groups such as the Beatles and the Rolling Stones also gained a worldwide following. Some British musicians combine modern styles with the music of their homelands. M.I.A., a singer-songwriter with family roots in Sri Lanka, blends hip-hop and South Asian styles and his music is enjoyed around the world.

FAMOUS BRITONS

George Frederic Handel
1685–1759

George Frederic Handel was born in Germany. He first came to London in 1710. A few years later Handel began to write music for King George I, who was also a German by birth. Handel eventually settled in England. His music is still played and enjoyed around the world, especially the *Messiah*. This piece about the life of Christ is often played before Christmas or Easter.

Educated and Informed

England is home to two of the world's best universities, Cambridge and Oxford. Although most people leave school able to read and write, much debate continues over the approach to learning and the content of the curriculum. The government-owned British Broadcasting Company (BBC) offers radio and television programmes across the UK, as well as a news website. The BBC is also a major global player in the media, and its television programmes and radio service are transmitted worldwide. Hundreds of private companies also offer radio and television services, and daily newspapers are published across the country.

GOING GLOBAL

Since 1932, the BBC World Service has provided news to dozens of countries around the world. At first only available on radio, the World Service now also offers Internet news in 27 languages, including Russian, Chinese, Swahili and French.

▼ *Founded in the twelfth century, Oxford University is one of the oldest – and one of the best – in the world.*

Sports

The modern forms of several ball sports were born in the UK, including association football (soccer), rugby, golf, table tennis and cricket. English footballers are known and respected all over the world, and many of them go to play for football clubs in other countries, where they are much in demand. In 1966, England's football team won the World Cup, football's greatest international competition. UK athletes have also performed well at the Olympics. London hosted the Summer Games in 1908, 1948 and 2012. High-quality sporting venues were built across London and elsewhere to accommodate the Olympic events.

▲ *This young rugby fan has painted his face as the English flag, a red cross on a white background.*

Art and entertainment

More than 400 years ago, William Shakespeare wrote plays featuring comedy, romance and history. Today he is read more often in English-speaking nations than any other writer. Since his time, Britons have continued to write books, plays and poems that are enjoyed around the world. Such classic tales as *Frankenstein*, *Robinson Crusoe* and *The Lord of the Rings* were written in the UK. In painting, J. M. W. Turner, Thomas Gainsborough and Francis Bacon are among internationally famous Britons.

FAMOUS BRITONS

J. K. Rowling
b. 1965

In 1996, J. K. Rowling published a fantasy story about Harry Potter, a boy studying to become a wizard, and later added six more books to the series. She has become one of the most successful modern writers, selling hundreds of millions of books around the world. Several films based on the *Harry Potter* series rank among the most popular of all time.

Economy and trade

Over the centuries, trade with other countries helped make the UK one of the wealthiest nations in the world. Although hard hit by the economic crisis that began in 2008, it is still the world's ninth-largest economy, with valuable resources and skilled workers.

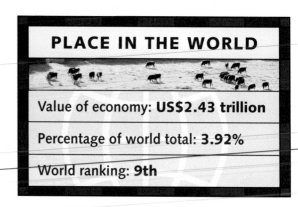

PLACE IN THE WORLD

Value of economy: **US$2.43 trillion**

Percentage of world total: **3.92%**

World ranking: **9th**

Goods and services

British factories make goods, including vehicles and medicines, that are exported all over the world. London is a global centre for another kind of industry – banking and financial services. Many international financial companies have their European headquarters in the City of London. In insurance, Lloyd's of London is world famous, doing business in more than 200 countries. There has recently been a move away from manufacturing, and financial companies and other services such as retail and healthcare employ about 80 per cent of the UK's workers.

▼ *The City, an area of just 2.5 sq km (1 sq mile), is London's main financial district.*

▲ Livestock farming is an important part of the UK economy, as meat products are a major export.

Farming

British farm and fishing products help feed people around the world. Industrialized farming allows just two per cent of the population to grow 60 per cent of the country's food. Top food exports include grains and meat products. However, the UK relies on other nations for some of its food, importing such goods as beverages, fruits and vegetables, and fish.

Natural resources

Oil found beneath the North Sea and the goods made from it are some of the UK's major exports, and natural gas is another North Sea resource. BP, based in London, is one of the world's largest energy companies. It searches the world for new sources of oil and natural gas. The UK also has large amounts of coal and other natural resources such as tin and limestone.

IT STARTED HERE

The Industrial Revolution

England was the birthplace of the Industrial Revolution. During the 1760s and 1770s, James Watt perfected a steam engine that powered equipment used to make textiles. Steam power and machines made it easier to produce a variety of goods more quickly and cheaply than ever, and their use spread around the world.

Tourism

Tourism is an important part of the UK economy, and the country attracts visitors from around the world. Over 30 million foreign tourists visited the UK in 2011, and they spent about £17 million. The foreign travellers and tourists from within the UK make tourism one of the country's major industries. More than 2.5 million people work in jobs tied to tourism.

IT'S A FACT!

The euro is the unit of currency for most EU nations. The UK, however, has chosen to keep its own currency, the pound. Denmark is the only other EU member that is not currently using the euro or planning to adopt it.

◀ *London is the UK's top tourist destination. Visitors enjoy modern attractions such as the London Eye, as well as the city's many historical sites.*

Renewable energy

The Industrial Revolution led to the vast use of oil, coal and natural gas as sources of power, and this meant that too much of these precious resources were used up. As reserves declined – and people realized the harm caused to the environment by burning them – production fell. The government now promotes the use of renewable sources of energy, such as wind and water power. The UK ranks eighth in the world in terms of wind power. Marine Current Turbines, of Bristol, England, is a world leader in building turbines to capture the energy produced by tides and ocean currents. However, the UK still falls behind many other nations in terms of total power generated by renewable resources. Its climate means it cannot harness solar power as much as sunnier countries such as the USA or those in the Mediterranean.

▲ *The UK already has several wind farms, including two huge ones off the coast of south-east England.*

Trade partners

The USA and Germany are the UK's major trading partners. Other top trading partners include the Netherlands, France, Belgium, China and Switzerland. Around fifty per cent of all UK exports are sold to countries in the European Union. To promote a healthy world economy, the UK belongs to several international organizations. The Group of Eight (G8) hosts meetings between the leaders of the world's most powerful industrial nations. The Group of 20 includes nations that are quickly expanding their economies, such as Brazil, India and China. The UK hosted a G20 meeting in 2009.

FAMOUS BRITONS

Sir Richard Branson
b. 1950

Richard Branson began his business career producing and selling music. He called his company the Virgin Group, and it soon expanded into many other areas. Today the company has 50,000 employees in 34 countries. Now a billionaire, Branson has given some of his wealth to international charities. He was knighted in 1999.

The United Kingdom is a constitutional monarchy, which means that although the queen is the head of state, the country is governed by the prime minister and parliament. Across the UK, the people choose who serves in parliament and on local councils.

The monarchy

For centuries, monarchs were the supreme rulers of England, Scotland and Wales. Over time, citizens gained a say in how the country should be run, by electing members of parliament. By the end of the seventeenth century, parliament had greater legal powers than the monarch. Despite this the monarch remains an important symbol for the UK, as well as ruling Commonwealth states such as Australia.

▼ *Prince Charles is heir to the throne of the UK and the countries of the Commonwealth.*

FAMOUS BRITONS

Prince Charles
b. 1948

Prince Charles, eldest son of Queen Elizabeth II and Prince Philip, is next in line to the throne of the UK. He is known for his work with several charities and his interest in environmental issues. In 2007, Prince Charles started the Rainforests Project to stop the cutting down of trees in the world's tropical rainforests.

Parliament

Parliament is divided into two parts, called houses. The House of Commons has 646 members, who are elected by voters. There are around 750 members of the House of Lords, who are mostly appointed by the monarch. Some hold their seats for life, while others can pass their seats on to their children when they die. Scotland also has its own parliament, while Wales and Northern Ireland have 'assemblies'. Each of these bodies passes laws for its particular region. Local governments, called councils, handle such issues as education, road repair and maintaining public spaces.

IT'S A FACT!

In 1215, English nobles forced King John to sign a document called the Magna Carta. In this, the king promised to protect some of the nobles' rights and gave them more power than they had ever had before. The Magna Carta is considered one of the world's most important documents in the creation of modern democratic government.

▼ *The Scottish parliament, established in 1998, is based in the capital Edinburgh.*

Parties and the prime minister

Most members of parliament and local leaders belong to political parties. The largest in the UK are the Conservatives, the Labour Party and the Liberal Democrats. The party with the most elected members in the House of Commons chooses the leader of the government, called the prime minister. The prime minister chooses other ministers to head different government departments. These departments handle such issues as defence, protecting the environment and foreign affairs. Many countries that were once part of the British Empire use a similar parliamentary government, including India, Barbados and Malaysia.

GLOBAL LEADER

Despite the global economic slowdown since 2008, the UK government continues to support a wide range of overseas aid projects. It hopes to lead by example, and encourages other countries to match its foreign aid budget. While most UK government departments have seen their budgets slashed, the Department for International Development's budget has actually grown.

◀ *No. 10 Downing Street contains the home and offices of the British prime minister. Here, former prime minister Gordon Brown greets the president of Pakistan and his daughter.*

As one of the permanent members of the United Nations (UN), the UK can veto, or overturn, any resolution passed by the council. In recent decades, the UK has used this power only a few times.

▲ *British troops have helped bring stability to Afghanistan, and several hundred have sacrificed their lives in the process.*

The United Nations

As a world leader, the UK plays an important role in several international organizations. The UK was one of the founding members of the United Nations, which today has almost 200 members. The British hold one of five permanent seats on the UN's most powerful body, the Security Council. The council actively tries to end disputes between member nations and keep peace around the world.

Military power

The UK is one of about 10 countries with nuclear weapons, although it has never used them in battle, relying instead on its army, navy and air force for defence. The UK – along with 27 other countries – is a member of the North Atlantic Treaty Organization (NATO). This group's original goal was to defend Europe and North America from invasion. Now, NATO sometimes sends troops around the world. As part of NATO, the UK has sent thousands of soldiers to Afghanistan to help fight the 'War on Terror'. The UK also supported the US-led invasion of Iraq in 2003.

The UK in 2020

Environmental issues, an ageing population and the rise in immigrant numbers are just some of the problems the UK will face in the near future. However, the government and the British people are already taking steps to address these issues.

Going green

The current push to 'go green' will change how Britons get their energy. There are government schemes that pay homeowners who use wind and solar power to generate their own electricity. All homes will also have new meters that measure how much power is used. People will know right away if they are using more power than usual so they can look for ways to cut back. The government will need to work hard to make sure the country is 'greener' in the future.

Still a world leader?

In the years ahead, skilled researchers in many industries could help the UK strengthen its economy. Several medical centres and universities are seeking to slow the effects of ageing, fight cancer and reduce the risk of heart disease and other deadly illnesses. New drugs and medical techniques could save lives and create jobs. However, it may take time to recover from the economic problems of the first decade of the 2000s.

▼ *There are already eco-villages such as BedZED in the UK, and in the future there may be more 'green' communities.*

▲ *The Notting Hill Carnival celebrates the UK's cultural diversity. More immigration in the future will enhance the country's multicultural nature.*

FAMOUS BRITONS

Diane Abbot, MP
b. 1953

The daughter of Jamaican immigrants, Diane Abbot made history in 1987 by becoming the first black woman to be elected as a Member of Parliament. Aside from her official duties, she uses her position to help fight racism and raise educational achievement levels amongst black children.

A changing population

As the population of the UK ages, it will also become more diverse. The number of non-white Britons has risen steadily since 2001, and some cities will have more non-white residents than whites by the 2020s. Non-whites, however, are not well represented in parliament. The major parties seek to have a more diverse government in the years to come. Attitudes and ideas from people of many backgrounds will help the UK face the challenges of the future.

Glossary

colony a territory under the immediate political control of a state.

democracy a type of government where people vote for the people they wish to represent them.

economy the financial system of a country or region, including how much money is made from the production and sale of goods and services.

emigration when someone leaves the country of their birth to settle in another country.

emissions gases that are given off during industrial processes or by vehicles.

ethnic group a group of people classed together according to their racial, national, linguistic or cultural origin or background.

export to send or transport products or materials abroad for sale or trade.

fossil fuels fuels made from the remains of plants and animals that died millions of years ago. Coal, oil and natural gas are all fossil fuels.

global warming the gradual rise in temperatures on the surface of the Earth caused by changes in the amount of greenhouse gases in the atmosphere.

greenhouse gas a gas that helps trap warmth in the atmosphere, which can contribute to global warming if too much is generated on Earth.

immigrant a person who has moved to another country to live.

import to bring in goods or materials from a foreign country for sale.

nuclear weapons bombs and other explosive weapons that get their power from nuclear reactions.

pollution spoiling the environment – such as the air or water – with man-made waste.

refugee someone who flees from war, oppression or persecution in search of refuge and safety.

resources things that are available to use, often to help develop a country's industry and economy. Resources could be minerals, workers (labour) or water.

rural relating to the countryside.

suburbs areas on the outskirts of cities that are less built-up than city centres.

terrorist a person who uses violence or causes fear, to try and change a political system or policy.

textiles cloth or fabric, usually made from weaving or knitting.

United Nations (UN) an organization of the world's countries formed in 1945 to promote peace throughout the world.

Further information

Books

London: A Time Traveller's Guide
by Moira Butterfield
(Franklin Watts, 2013)

Britain the Facts series
(Franklin Watts, 2008)

The United Kingdom (Discover Countries) by Tim Atkinson
(Wayland, 2012)

Britain Since World War II series
(Franklin Watts, 2007)

The UK Today
by Michael Gallagher
(Franklin Watts, 2007)

Life in Post-War Britain
by Brian Williams
(Heinemann Library, 2009)

Monarchy
by Christopher Riches
(Franklin Watts, 2008)

A Visit to the United Kingdom
by Rachel Bell
(Heinemann, 2008)

Websites

https://www.cia.gov/library/publications/ the-world-factbook/geos/UK.html
CIA World Factbook – United Kingdom. Includes a map and current statistics on the United Kingdom and its people.

www.bbc.co.uk/news/world-europe-18023389
The BBC offers facts on the country and links to recent news stories from the country.

www.gov.uk/
The official website of the British government, offering information on daily life and links to every major government agency and department.

http://www.statistics.gov.uk/hub/index.html
For the latest national and local statistics on population, economics, and more.

Every effort has been made by the publisher to ensure that these websites contain no inappropriate or offensive material. However, because of the nature of the Internet, it is impossible to guarantee that the contents of these sites will not be altered. We strongly advise that Internet access is supervised by a responsible adult.

Index

Numbers in **bold** indicate pictures